Jim Cliff

Fallacious Trump

The Donald J. Trump Guide to Logical Fallacies

Also by Jim Cliff

Covfefe! Donald Trump's Craziest Tweets
The Best Words: The Collected Wisdom of Donald J. Trump
The Shoulders of Giants: A Jake Abraham Mystery
Bad Memory: A Jake Abraham Mystery Novella
The Ultimate Friends Quiz Book
The Ultimate TV Quiz Book: The '80s
The Ultimate TV Quiz Book: The '90s

FALLACIOUS TRUMP
THE DONALD J. TRUMP GUIDE TO LOGICAL FALLACIES

Copyright © 2017 Jim Cliff

All rights reserved.
ISBN: 9781976933929
Published by Antbear Books, 2018, Colchester, UK

FOR TRUMP, THAT HE MAY LEARN

CONTENTS

WHAT IS A LOGICAL FALLACY?

A logical fallacy is an error in reasoning that makes an argument invalid. By learning to spot them in other people's arguments, and in our own, we can get better at backing up our claims, and make it harder for others to fool us.

In a valid argument, the conclusion that the speaker makes naturally follows on from the statements (premises) they present to support it. If the argument is logically valid and the premises are true, then we can safely assume that the conclusion is true.

Sometimes, though, an illogical argument seems compelling at first glance. This might be because someone is deliberately trying to mislead us, or they might be accidentally using an invalid argument because they haven't spotted what they're doing themselves.

Many of these arguments are so common that we can break them down into groups to make it easier to identify them and explain why they're invalid.

Is this just nitpicking?

Identifying logical fallacies isn't about being pedantic and scoring points over someone you're arguing with. Logical fallacies can make false or unsupported arguments seem more convincing, thereby deceiving the listener. If you want to avoid being deceived, knowing what to look for can be helpful.

Just spotting a fallacy doesn't prove the person is not telling the truth - it just means their conclusion isn't supported by their evidence. There may be other evidence that does in fact support the conclusion. In fact, claiming someone's conclusion is wrong just because they've used a fallacy is called the Fallacy Fallacy.

Finally, if you identify a fallacy in someone's argument, it's not OK just to say 'That's a Straw Man Fallacy' and look smug. Instead, use your understanding of why their argument is invalid to challenge their conclusion, and help them see why it's not supported by the evidence.

WHY TRUMP?

Let me make it very clear: Trump is by no means alone in using logical fallacies. It's not a Trump thing, it's not a Republican thing, it's not even a politician thing. Everybody does it from time to time, even me.

So why am I picking on Trump? Well, he is particularly prolific in his use of bad arguments. His bombastic, unapologetic, off-the-cuff style of speaking, coupled with his tendency to make things up means that he provides a lot of examples on a regular basis.

Also, I think it's funny.

AD HOMINEM
(AKA personal attack, name calling)

Person A believes X, but he's an idiot. Therefore, X must be false.

Ad Hominem is Latin for 'to the man' and describes an argument where the focus of the attack is not on the views a person holds but on the person themselves. It is an attempt to distract from the matter at hand by introducing irrelevant details aimed at discrediting the individual.

For example, when Senator Richard Blumenthal said that the investigation into potential collusion between Trump and Russia must be pursued, Trump's defense was a typical Ad Hominem fallacy:

10

Trump didn't defend his position, he simply attacked. The fact that Senator Blumenthal lied about his military career is completely irrelevant to the question of whether collusion should be investigated.

Similarly in an interview on *Fox and Friends* in 2017, interviewer Pete Hegseth asked
"How do you overcome that, when someone like Senator Warren, Senator Elizabeth Warren literally says people are going to die because of President Trump's health care bill?"

Trump's response didn't address the Health Care Bill at all, preferring instead to attack Senator Warren:

> Well I actually think she's a hopeless case. I call her Pocahontas and that's an insult to Pocahontas. I actually think that she is just somebody that's got a lot of hatred, a lot of anger.

Again, whether or not Senator Warren has Native American heritage is totally irrelevant to the dangers inherent in Trump's Health Care Bill

Trump just loves insulting people, and if he had an above fourth grade vocabulary, he might be pretty good at it. However, it's important to remember that an insult is not the same as an Ad Hominem fallacy. It's not a fallacy to say something mean about someone. It only becomes a fallacy if you claim that their argument is wrong *because* of the negative attribute you ascribed to them

When Meryl Streep used her Golden Globes platform to point out that it's not OK to make fun of disabled people, she didn't mention Trump by name. But she didn't have to. In his Twitter reply, he called her *"one of the most overrated actresses in Hollywood"* but he also defended his position, claiming that he never mocked the reporter. Since he didn't claim that she was wrong *because* she was overrated technically this isn't an Ad Hominem fallacy.

For the record, Trump did mock that disabled reporter. Because of course he did. He did it into a working microphone, in front of a camera he knew was on, in a room full of people.

APPEAL TO FEAR/EMOTION

(AKA argumentum ad metum, scare tactics, argument from adverse consequences)

X is really scary, so we should do Y.

People often make decisions based on emotion rather than logic, so appealing to that emotion can be a very useful technique when you're trying to persuade someone. However, to be part of an effective logical argument emotion has to be used to back up the argument, rather than form the primary basis of the argument.

In the 3rd Presidential debate between Donald Trump and Hillary Clinton, Trump said the following:

Now, you can say that that's OK and Hillary can say that that's OK. But it's not OK with me, because based on what she's saying, and based on where she's going, and where she's been, you can take the baby and rip the baby out of the womb in the ninth month on the final day. And that's not acceptable.

Even if we ignore the egregious Straw Man fallacy Trump is committing here, and the fact that he's confused abortion with childbirth, it's clear that he is making his argument based entirely on emotion. By using the phrase *"rip the baby out of the womb,"* and suggesting that it might happen even up to the final day of pregnancy he is trying to create outrage and disgust in the audience.

If Hillary Clinton was suggesting that abortions should happen so late in the pregnancy (if that was even possible) there would be plenty of good logical arguments why that would be a terrible idea. By appealing to emotion instead of making an argument Trump has simply attempted to damage Hillary's reputation by association with a frightening procedure.

Appealing to fear is a common technique of Trump's. In a speech in Charleston in 2015 Trump defended his plan to ban Muslims from travelling to the USA by saying:

We can't live like this. It's gonna get worse and worse. You're gonna have more World Trade Centers - it's gonna get worse and worse, folks.

The fact is that security experts agree that the travel ban will be ineffective in preventing terrorists from entering the United States and be likely to encourage exactly the kind of resentment and isolation that in some cases fuels support for radical religious fundamentalists. Rather than addressing these issues and making a positive argument in favor of his travel ban, Trump instead seeks to instill fear so that people vote for his strategy without thinking about whether it will actually work.

ARGUMENTUM AD NAUSEAM
(AKA proof by assertion, argument by repetition)

X is true. X is true. X is true.

The Ad Nauseam logical fallacy refers to a situation where someone asserts a claim repeatedly, often even after the claim has been debunked, in the hope that people will start to believe it through sheer repetition and that people will get sick of trying to refute it so they will simply give up.

To be honest, it's hardly fair even calling this an argument; it's really just 'pretending nobody has noticed that you're lying'.

During the campaign Donald Trump was very fond of saying that his tax cuts would be the biggest since Ronald Reagan.

In May of 2017 Trump changed his mind and decided that his tax cut would be the biggest in the history of the United States. He said as much in an interview with Bloomberg on May the 1st.

The regulation cuts are going to have an even bigger impact than the massive tax cuts. And this is the biggest tax cut in history. This is bigger than Reagan. Remember we used to say, "The biggest since Reagan"?

Later that week he repeated this assertion in a speech where he said:

As you know we put our tax plan in, it's a massive tax cut, the biggest tax cut in the history of our country.

Over the next six months Trump would make this same claim a total of 40 times. At no point during this time was the claim true. According to the fact checkers at *The Washington Post* and *PolitiFact*, Trump's tax cut was beaten by Reagan's, two of Obama's, and two of Truman's tax cuts. This was pointed out at multiple times after Trump started making this claim but rather than adjust his position he simply continued asserting the same thing.

Trump was very excited by the size of his Electoral College victory, often claiming it was one of the biggest in history (it was in the bottom third), but more than anything else, he likes to talk about how hard it is for a Republican to win the Electoral College at all, due to the huge advantage the system gives to Democrats. This started with a speech in Louisville back in March 2017, when he said:

> *And, you know, for the Republicans, the Electoral College was very, very hard, very hard to win.*

Later that day he tweeted:

Donald J. Trump ✓
@realDonaldTrump

Following ⌄

The Democrats made up and pushed the Russian story as an excuse for running a terrible campaign. Big advantage in Electoral College & lost!

3:49 AM - 20 Mar 2017

And he would go on to brag about overcoming this huge advantage 17 times over the next seven months, frequently claiming that it was almost impossible for a Republican to win the Electoral College:

> *The reason they [Democrats] should've won it is, the Electoral College is almost impossible for a Republican to win.*

Of course, this is nonsense. Not only have the Republicans won the Electoral College vote 8 times in the last 60 years (compared to 6 wins for Democrats), half of those Republicans won a larger share of the Electoral College votes than Trump. Twice since 2000, the Democrats have won the popular vote and lost the Electoral College vote.

We know that Trump watches a large amount of TV, especially about when it's about himself, so it's reasonable to assume he has seen one or more instances of this obvious lie being debunked, but it hasn't affected his determination to keep repeating the lie.

Argument from Authority
(AKA argumentum ad verecundiam, appeal to false authority)

X must be true because Celebrity A says it is.

This is more accurately called the Argument from Improper or False Authority. After all, it's entirely valid to support your argument by invoking a *relevant* authority like, say, climate scientists opinions on climate change.

However, when the authority you invoke is not an authority on the subject at hand, or objectively not reliable or trustworthy, you are committing a fallacy. A very common form of this is the Appeal to Celebrity, which is why adverts constantly try to get us to associate products with famous people we like. But even if Kendall Jenner did drink Pepsi, would that make it a superior soft drink?

Trump's own celebrity is of course a large part of his appeal, but he didn't hesitate to announce the fact that Tom Brady endorsed him during the campaign.

> *Tom Brady likes me – what can I tell you? I think if Tom Brady likes you, you're in pretty good shape.*

Tom Brady may be the Greatest of All Time on the football field, but does he know any more than you do about what would make someone a good President? How much weight should we give his opinion when deciding who to vote for?

I should reiterate here that Trump is certainly not alone in capitalizing on his celebrity endorsements - all politicians and pretty much all big companies do the exact same thing.

At least Tom Brady is an authority on something, though. Some 'authorities' are just unreliable or untrustworthy. In March of 2016, Trump claimed on *Fox and Friends* that Ted Cruz's father knew Lee Harvey Oswald:

> *His father was with Lee Harvey Oswald prior to Oswald's being — you know, shot. I mean, the whole thing is ridiculous. What is this, right prior to his being shot, and nobody even brings it up. They don't even talk about that.*

When Trump was called on to defend these insane comments, he invoked the sketchiest of authorities:

> *Now I don't know what it was, exactly, but it was a major story in a major publication and it was picked up by many other publications.*

The 'major publication' Trump saw the story in was *The National Enquirer*. The tabloid that claimed that Justice Antonin Scalia was murdered by a prostitute who was hired by the CIA to assassinate him by injecting poison into his buttocks. The tabloid that *mediabiasfactcheck.com* describes as *"the original fake news media outlet that profits by selling fake news."*

ARGUMENT FROM IGNORANCE
(AKA argumentum ad ignorantium, negative proof)

You haven't proved X is true. Therefore, X must be false.

The Argument from Ignorance fallacy describes a situation where someone claims a proposition to be true simply because it has not yet been proven to be false. Obviously if an outlandish claim is made and it cannot immediately be proven to be false that does not mean it should automatically be assumed to be true.

In November of 2016 Donald Trump tweeted the following outlandish claim:

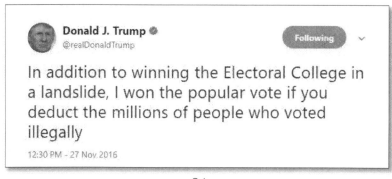

Donald J. Trump @realDonaldTrump
Following

In addition to winning the Electoral College in a landslide, I won the popular vote if you deduct the millions of people who voted illegally

12:30 PM - 27 Nov. 2016

CNN senior White House correspondent Jeff Zeleny called this claim *"blatant and baseless"* and pointed out that Trump has offered no evidence to back it up.

In response, Trump started tweeting about CNN and retweeted a 16-year-old from California who tweeted:

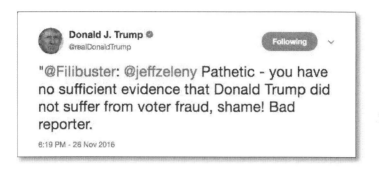

Donald J. Trump ✓
@realDonaldTrump

"@Filibuster: @jeffzeleny Pathetic - you have no sufficient evidence that Donald Trump did not suffer from voter fraud, shame! Bad reporter.

6:19 PM - 28 Nov 2016

Trump is the one making the outlandish claim here - the idea that over 3 million illegal votes lost him the popular vote. This requires some evidence. It is not enough simply to say you haven't proved there wasn't any voter fraud

Similarly when Trump was called on to defend his claim that Ted Cruz's father worked with Lee Harvey Oswald Trump offered the following evidence:

All I was doing was referring to a picture that was reported in a magazine, and I think they didn't deny it. I don't think anybody denied it.

Even if Trump was correct that the story had not been denied, that does not make the story true.

In fact, almost two weeks before Trump's claiming this, the Cruz campaign's communications director, Alice Stewart, said: *"The story is false; that is not Rafael in the picture."*

The day before Trump defended himself with this claim, Cruz said: *"This morning Donald Trump went on national television and attacked my father. Donald Trump alleges that my dad was involved in assassinating JFK. Let's be clear, this is nuts. This is not a reasonable position, this is just kooky."*

The same day, Rafael Cruz said that the links insinuated between him and Oswald were *"ludicrous." "I was never in New Orleans at that time,"* he said.

ARGUMENT FROM PERSONAL INCREDULITY
(AKA appeal to common sense)

I can't understand how X could be true. Therefore it must be false.

The Argument from Personal Incredulity describes a situation where someone dismisses a claim for no other reason than they find it difficult to believe. In fact, the person may be having trouble believing something simply because it doesn't conform to how they currently think, or even that they simply don't understand some element of the claim. However, rather than asking for more information or an explanation, the claim is dismissed as false because it seems unlikely to them.

In February 2017 *The Washington Post* reported that National Security Advisor General Mike Flynn had discussed sanctions with Russian Ambassador Sergey Kislyak, and cited 'nine current and former officials' as sources for the story.

Trump was skeptical, saying:

Because they have no sources, they just make 'em up when there are none. I saw one story recently where they said, "Nine people have confirmed." There're no nine people. I don't believe there was one or two people. Nine people.

The fact that Trump doesn't believe *The Washington Post* had nine sources (or even one or two) doesn't make it any less true, but he asserts *"There're no nine people,"* with no evidence but his personal incredulity. Frankly, given the unprecedented scale of leaks from the White House during 2017, it doesn't even seem that unlikely - some stories cite twenty or more sources from inside Trump's administration.

At a rally in Phoenix in August 2017, Trump expressed his inability to believe that there had ever been a more effective President than him:

I don't believe that any president has accomplished as much as this president in the first six or seven months. I really don't believe it.

It's obvious to anyone with access to Google and twenty seconds to spare that every President in living memory accomplished far more than Trump in the first six months. The fact that The Donald really doesn't believe this has no effect on reality.

ARGUMENT FROM POPULARITY

(AKA argumentum ad populum, appeal to the masses, bandwagon fallacy)

Everyone believes X. Therefore, X must be true.

Trump likes to talk about 'many people' doing, thinking or saying something, to give the impression that whatever they are doing, thinking or saying is correct. In doing so, he is arguing from the popularity of an idea, rather than using evidence to show the idea is true. This is an extremely common fallacy. After all, if a lot of people believe something, it must be true, right?

Despite the (ironic) popularity of this fallacy, it's quite easy to refute. The fact that billions of people believe Jesus was the son of God is a compelling argument until someone points out that billions of other people believe Jesus wasn't the son of God.

When Trump claimed the only reason he didn't win the popular vote was massive voter fraud in the election, and then backed his claim up with an Argument from Popularity, even Bill O'Reilly called him out on it:

O'Reilly: But if you say for example that there are three million illegal aliens who voted and then, you don't have the data to back it up, some people are going to say, that is irresponsible for a President to say that. Is there any validity?
Trump: Well, many people have come out and said I am right. You know that.
O'Reilly: I know but you have to have the data to back that up.

O'Reilly: So, you think you're going to be proven correct in that statement?
Trump: Well, I think I already have. A lot of people have come out and said that I am right.

When Bill "You can't explain why the tide goes in" O'Reilly questions your logic, it's time to take a long hard look at yourself.

In the run up to the election, Trump tweeted this:

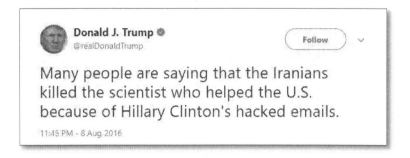

It would have been more accurate to tweet that many people were retweeting this claim, which stemmed from a single source - a tweet from the Drudge Report asking, in all caps, CLINTON EMAIL LED TO EXECUTION IN IRAN?

Even if many people were saying this, it doesn't make it any more true. In actual fact, Shahram Amiri, the Iranian scientist in question, was outed as a CIA spy by ABC News in March of 2010 and the story was widely reported in other sources for months before Amiri was ever mentioned in emails connected to Hillary Clinton's private server in July of that year.

Sean Spicer, Sarah Huckabee-Sanders and Hope Hicks have all repeatedly said that Trump's tweets *'speak for themselves'*. This one certainly does:

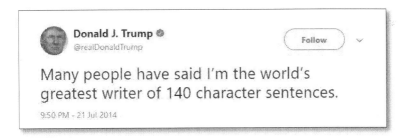

I'm going to go out on a limb and say that nobody has ever said this about Trump. And again, even if they had, it doesn't make it true.

ASSOCIATION FALLACY
(AKA guilt by association)

Person A believes X, but Person A is connected to Person B, who is bad. Therefore, X must be false.

The Association Fallacy occurs when a person or information source is dismissed because of their connection to, or their similarity to another person or source which is already viewed negatively for some established reason.

For example, in the Presidential debates, Trump spoke repeatedly about Hillary's husband, former President Bill Clinton. In response to Hillary's remarks on immigration reform, he said:

34

The NAFTA deal signed by her husband is one of the worst deals ever made of any kind, signed by anybody. It's a disaster.

This is a fallacy because whether or not her husband was good at making trade deals is irrelevant to Hillary Clinton's immigration policies or her stance on the border wall. The Association Fallacy is a type of Ad Hominem attack, in that the focus is intentionally shifted away from the argument and onto the person.

Of course, it goes both ways, and so we must not assume that simply because Trump chose racist homophobe Steve Bannon as his Chief Strategist, that Trump himself is a racist homophobe. Fortunately, we have so much corroborating evidence that we have no need to make such an assumption.

BEGGING THE QUESTION
(AKA petitio principii)

X is true because X is true.

Begging the Question is one of those phrases that has come to mean something different over time. Colloquially, it is used to mean 'raising the question', but the original meaning is the one invoked by this fallacy, and it's fun to point out that people are using the phrase wrong, once you've explained that tomatoes are fruits and reminded them on the difference between poisonous and venomous.

For the purposes of the fallacy, Begging the Question means assuming the conclusion of your argument to be true, and using that assumption within the argument. It is a form of Circular Reasoning with even less reasoning than usual.

Most people will never produce a completely pure example of Begging the Question, because it's such a bizarre way to try to convince anybody of anything, but of course The Donald can be relied upon to provide an archetypal specimen in his now legendary Press Conference in February 2017:

Well the leaks are real. You're the one that wrote about them and reported them, I mean the leaks are real. You know what they said, you saw it and the leaks are absolutely real. The news is fake because so much of the news is fake.

"The news is fake because so much of the news is fake".

It's almost sublime.

CHERRY PICKING
(AKA selective observation, ignoring inconvenient data)

If we ignore all the data against it, this piece of data shows X is true.

Cherry Picking is a logical fallacy in which the arguer ignores a large amount of evidence which casts doubt on their claim, carefully selecting only the parts which make their claim sound plausible. Where there is controversy on an issue, data to support both sides, or ambiguous reports which can be interpreted in different ways, it is entirely natural for people to favor the evidence that confirms their beliefs. However, when there is a preponderance of data on one side, or unambiguous facts some will still choose to select information that misrepresents the true situation or take elements out of context in order to mislead. These people are Cherry Picking.

In his first address to a Joint Session of Congress in February 2017, Mr. Trump managed an impressive total of three Cherry Picked statements within just 27 words:

Tonight, as I outline the next steps we must take as a country, we must honestly acknowledge the circumstances we inherited. 93 million Americans are out of the labor force. Over 43 million people are now living in poverty. And over 43 million Americans are on food stamps.

Based on the sentence that precedes them, Trump is very clearly trying to use these three statistics to show how bad things got under Obama. And sure, without any context, they sound bad.

But how about that context?

The 93 million "out of the labor force" statistic was actually a bit low due to the fact it was out of date. The most recent data at the time was from August 2016, and it put the figure at 94.4 million.

"Out of the labor force" sounds like a fancy way of saying "unemployed", but actually it covers a number of groups.

Of that 94.4 million, over 44 million Americans were retired, and 13.2 million were still in school and college. 15.3 million were disabled and unable to work, and 13.3 million were stay-at-home parents.

In fact only 7.8 million Americans were out of work and looking for a job. This represents an unemployment rate of under 5% - the result of a steady rise in job growth under Obama since late 2010 when the unemployment rate hit 10%.

As for the 43 million Americans living in poverty, and the same number on food stamps, these were indeed accurate statistics at the time. However, in both cases these numbers are the lowest since late 2010 at which time there were nearly 49 million Americans living in poverty and around 48 million on food stamps.

Both metrics improved dramatically under Obama's leadership. But of course, that's a bit of context that The Donald wants to stay well clear of.

EQUIVOCATION

Person A believes X, but X can also mean something bad. Therefore, Person A is wrong.

The Equivocation fallacy relies on using a word with more than one meaning to set up a misleading argument. Often the word will be used in one sense in the premise, and in the other sense in the conclusion, implying that because the word is the same, the meanings are the same.

For example, a tweet attacking Hillary Clinton was retweeted by Trump early on in the campaign:

Donald J. Trump ⊜
@realDonaldTrump

"@mplefty67: If Hillary Clinton can't satisfy her husband what makes her think she can satisfy America?" @realDonaldTrump #2016president"

4/16/15, 5:22 PM

The word 'satisfy' is clearly being used to mean two separate things here. Even if we assumed that Hillary Clinton was indeed unable to satisfy (i.e. be sexually sufficient for) Bill, this would have no bearing on her ability to satisfy (i.e. be a good President of) America.

FALSE DILEMMA
(AKA false dichotomy, either/or fallacy, black and white fallacy)

If X isn't true then Y must be. There are no other options.

The False Dilemma fallacy is depressingly common, and quite easy to spot. It occurs when someone suggests or implies there are only two possible choices or outcomes, and if you don't choose one then the other is inevitable.

This is not a fallacy if there *are* in fact only two choices - whether the limiting factor is created artificially (e.g. *"you can either have steak or vegetarian lasagna"*) or by nature/logic (e.g. *"this lasagna either has meat in it or it doesn't"*)

However, in real life there are often multiple options or outcomes and it is a fallacy to suggest that only two exist when in fact there are others.

During his weekly video address to the American people in June 2017, Trump said the following regarding a bill to stop government funds going to sanctuary cities:

This legislation presents a simple choice: either vote to save and protect American lives, or vote to shield and comfort criminal aliens who threaten innocent lives and they've been shielded too long.

While this is an Appeal to Fear, it's also definitely a False Dilemma. Saving American lives or shielding and comforting criminal aliens are not the only two options. There are already plenty of laws against all the kinds of crimes that 'criminal aliens' might be committing - they are not shielded or comforted, they are arrested.

Meanwhile even if we accepted that withdrawing funds from sanctuary cities saves American lives, it is much more complicated than that. It disadvantages everyone in those cities by reducing the resources of the local government.

And if sanctuary cities start cooperating fully with ICE, then otherwise law-abiding undocumented people will be afraid to contact the authorities if they have information about a crime, or if they need help themselves.

By oversimplifying this complex issue into two choices - save lives or shield criminals - Trump is being disingenuous and fallacious. There may be good arguments for passing the legislation, but this isn't one of them.

FAULTY ANALOGY
(AKA weak analogy)

X is like Y in one respect. Y is bad. Therefore X is bad.

The fallacy of the Faulty Analogy is committed when you assume that because two things are alike in one way, then they are alike in all ways.

Before taking office, Trump appeared to believe that running the country was like running a business. In a speech at the Republican Convention in July 2016, he said:

I have made billions of dollars in business making deals - now I'm going to make our country rich again. Using the greatest business people in the world, which our country has, I am going to turn our bad trade agreements into great trade agreements.

Sure, there are some parallels - both countries and businesses make deals with other countries or businesses; there is money involved, there is a person in charge, etc.

However, assuming that this means a country can be run like a business is fallacious because there are also lots of differences which are just as important if not more so. For example, a business is run for profit, and consumers are able to choose which business they want to buy products from. A country is not run for profit, but for the good of its people, and the 'consumer' doesn't have a choice whether to pay the country or not, they will pay taxes whether they like it or not.

Even comparing things that seem very analogous can cause problems if we do not also consider the differences. In the 3rd Presidential Debate, Trump tried to suggest that the USA was failing because other countries' economies were growing faster:

So I just left some high representatives of India. They're growing at 8 percent. China is growing at 7 percent. And that for them is a catastrophically low number.

We are growing—our last report came out—and it's right around the 1 percent level. And I think it's going down.

At first this seems like a reasonable comparison - China and India must be doing better than America if their economy is growing so much faster. However, once you consider the differences between these countries it becomes obvious that this is exactly what we should expect. Developing countries should grow faster than developed ones! As India and China go through all the processes that help increase efficiency, from basic industrialization in some areas through to the adoption of new technology in others, fast economic growth is inevitable. In America, most of those advances have already happened. Growth will continue as incremental improvements are made, but that growth will necessarily be slower.

To suggest this shows that other countries are more successful or run more efficiently is to use a Faulty Analogy.

GENETIC FALLACY
(AKA fallacy of origins)

Person A believes X. I don't like Person A. Therefore X
must be wrong.

The Genetic Fallacy doesn't have anything to do with genes.
Rather, it relates to the 'genesis', or origin, of an argument.

When someone commits the Genetic Fallacy they are basing
their decision about whether a claim is true or false on who
is making the claim, or where it originated.

For example, way back in 2013 Trump tweeted the
following:

Like many Trump statements, this is pretty hard to parse - given his vocal opposition to both Obamacare and the concept of global warming; it's not entirely clear which he is using to denigrate the other. Let's assume, for the sake of argument, that this is an anti-climate change tweet, although it works the same either way.

Trump seems to be suggesting that because the source (in this case the Obama administration) 'gave you' something bad (Obamacare), then anything else they give you must also be bad. Now if we pretend for a moment that the Obama administration 'gave' us the concept of global warming (we must ignore over a century of climate science to manage this, but whatever) then we can see Trump is not basing his argument against global warming on anything other than who is claiming it exists. This, of course, has no bearing on the truth of the claim.

In June of 2016, Trump was interviewed on CNN about the class-action lawsuit against Trump University. He said:

> **Trump:** This judge is giving us unfair rulings. Now, I say. 'Why?' Well, I'm building a wall, OK? And it's a wall between Mexico. Not another country.
> **Jake Tapper:** But he's not from Mexico. He's from Indiana.
> **Trump:** He's of Mexican heritage and he's very proud of it.

In claiming that Judge Gonzalo Curiel was ruling against him because his parents originally came from Mexico, Trump committed the Genetic Fallacy - there is no attempt to argue the facts of the case, or give details of why the rulings were unfair. Instead it is deemed enough to say that the judge's Mexican heritage is the reason for the rulings, so they must be unfair.

Of course, every good critical thinker knows that it's important to consider the source when evaluating a claim, so how does that fit with the Genetic Fallacy?

Actually, these ways of thinking might be more compatible than they at first appear. It is not good reasoning to assume that someone who has been wrong before will be wrong every time they make a claim, or that because someone is biased, they aren't telling the truth.

However, this does not mean that the reliability, expertise, bias or relevance of a source should be dismissed when verifying the information from that source.

For example, when Donald Trump says that CNN's ratings are 'way down', it would be fallacious to assume he's wrong just because we know how much he hates CNN.

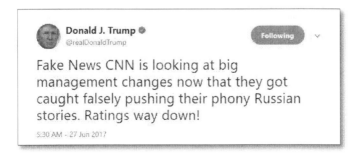

And it would also be fallacious to trust CNN's refutation of this without considering that they, too, have a reason to embellish the truth:

However, when CNN's argument is supported by data from Nielsen, an independent and well-respected organization with expertise in evaluating ratings, it is reasonable to assume this data is correctly precisely *because* of the credentials of the source.

CNN Ratings	Primetime, Total Viewers	Primetime, 25-54	Total Day, Total Viewers	Total Day, 25-54
2017 Q2	1,055,000	371,000	788,000	263,000
2016 Q2	959,000	312,000	627,000	188,000
2015 Q2	560,000	195,000	430,000	138,000
2014 Q2	459,000	156,000	341,000	105,000
2013 Q2	666,000	228,000	475,000	161,000

Similarly, when Trump said this about how Obama treated a protester at a rally in Fayetteville:

He was talking to the protester — screaming at him, really screaming at him. By the way, if I spoke the way Obama spoke to that protester, they would say, "He became unhinged! He became —" You have to go back and look and study. And see what happened. They never moved the camera. And he spent so much time screaming at this protester, and frankly, it was a disgrace.

It would be fallacious to assume, just because Trump is prone to making stuff up, that this whole description was huge lie. If we make such an assumption based purely on Trump's history of blatantly saying untrue things and his known hatred of Obama, we are committing the Genetic Fallacy.

Fortunately, we don't have to make this assumption, because the video of the event shows that Obama didn't scream at the protester, but in fact urged the crowd to respect him and his right to free speech. Here's what Obama said:

"Everybody sit down and be quiet for a second. You've got an older gentleman who is supporting his candidate. He's not doing nothing. You don't have to worry about him.

First of all, we live in a country that respects free speech.

Second of all, it looks like maybe he might have served in our military, and we ought to respect that. Third of all, he was elderly — and we've got to respect our elders.
And fourth of all, don't boo. Vote."

HASTY GENERALIZATION
(AKA argument from small numbers, leaping to conclusions)

X is true in very specific circumstances. Therefore, X is always true.

The fallacy of Hasty Generalization is committed when an assumption is made based on too little information. It may, for example, be that a small sample of a large group has been observed, and the properties of this sample are assumed to be present in the larger group.

This is fallacious because we don't know how representative the sample is of the larger group. Statistics based on small sample sizes aren't reliable, and can be misleading, so they shouldn't be relied upon when making generalizations.

Way back in 2015, in Trump's announcement speech, he hastily generalized about Mexicans:

When Mexico sends its people, they're not sending their best. They're not sending you. They're not sending you. They're sending people that have lots of problems, and they're bringing those problems with us. They're bringing drugs. They're bringing crime. They're rapists. And some, I assume, are good people.

Trump can (and frequently does) point out individual cases of illegal Mexican immigrants committing crimes. However, to then generalize about the entire group is fallacious.

It also happens to be wrong. Plenty of studies show that the level of criminal activity among illegal immigrants is very low compared to the general US population - a by-product perhaps of the fact that it is unwise to attract police attention if you are in the country illegally.

For example, according to the Public Policy Institute of California, among the non-incarcerated population of men aged 18-40 (the most commonly incarcerated group) in California, 17.2% are Mexican-born non-US-citizens. Among the prison population in this age group, only 2.9% are Mexican-born non-US-citizens.

Mexicans are not 'bringing crime' to the US. Their presence actually reduces the overall average crime rate.

HYPERBOLIC FALLACY
(AKA inductive hyperbole)

X is truer than anything else ever

When someone supports their argument by making a statement that is significantly more emphatic than can possibly be supported by evidence, they may be committing the Hyperbolic Fallacy.

As a rule a hyperbole is not meant to be taken literally. When someone says they had the worst morning ever, you know they are being dramatic rather than literal.

However, when someone uses hyperbole to defend or bolster their position in the absence of other evidence, their reasoning is not sound, because it is not possible to support such an extreme view with evidence - and often there is easily available refuting evidence.

President Trump is the best at using this fallacy - he's tremendous at it. For example, when Gold Star widow Myeshia Johnson claimed that The Donald couldn't even remember her late husband's name when he called her to offer his condolences, Trump said she was wrong, and to prove it, claimed to have:

One of the great memories of all time.

During his commencement speech at the US Coastguard Academy, Trump took the time to tell everyone:

No politician in history -- and I say this with great surety -- has been treated worse or more unfairly.

Trump presumably forgot (among countless other examples of worse treatment) that four US Presidents were actually assassinated.

This may in fact be Trump's favorite fallacy. Here is a very abridged list of just a few things that the President has claimed makes him so great:

"There's nobody bigger or better at the military than I am" - O'Reilly Factor, June 2015

"I am the least racist person you've ever interviewed" - remarks to the press, Jan 2018 (although Trump has made this claim on at least five other occasions).

"Nobody loves the Bible more than I do" - Rally in Sparks NV, Feb 2016

"Nobody's better to people with disabilities than me" - Rally in Daytona Beach FL, Aug 2016

"There's nobody that understands the horror of nuclear better than me" - Atlanta GA, June 2016

"Nobody has more respect for women than I do" - 2nd and 3rd Presidential debates, and multiple tweets

"Nobody's ever had crowds like Trump has had" - Press conference, early Jan 2017

"Nobody in the history of this country has ever known so much about infrastructure as Donald Trump" - New York, July 2016

"I think nobody knows more about taxes than I do, maybe in the history of the world" - AP interview, May 2016

IGNORATIO ELENCHI
(AKA missing the point, irrelevant conclusion)

Person A: Do you think X is true?
Person B: Here's some evidence that Y is true.
(Y is an unrelated or tangentially related issue).

This fallacy, sometimes called 'Missing the Point' is committed when someone provides evidence refuting or proving a point which is irrelevant to the issue at hand. This can often be a quite effective distraction, but as it does not address the real question, it remains fallacious.

In his press conference following the Charlottesville protests and killing of Heather Heyer, Trump was asked to clarify whether he felt the press was treating white supremacists unfairly. He started by saying some of the people there were not neo-Nazis, and then pointed out:

I don't know if you know, they had a permit. The other group didn't have a permit. So I only tell you this. There are two sides to a story.

Even if that was true (it wasn't - the counter-protesters did have a permit) it is hardly the point. The press were trying to give Trump the opportunity to condemn Nazis, and instead he focused on paperwork.

INCONSISTENT COMPARISON
(AKA false comparison, faulty comparison, apples and oranges)

If we compare one aspect of X with a completely different aspect of Y, we can see X is better than Y

When supporting your claims by comparing two things, it's important to be consistent in terms of what you're actually comparing. By doing so you can ensure it is a fair comparison and your point can be supported. If you are not fair when setting up the parameters, and you end up comparing the two in different ways, you are engaging in the fallacy of Inconsistent Comparison.

At the World Economic Forum in Davos, in January 2018, Trump claimed a huge success on one of his campaign pledges:

I pledged to eliminate two unnecessary regulations for every one new regulation. We have succeeded beyond our highest expectations. Instead of two-for-one, we have cut 22 burdensome regulations for every one new rule.

This claim is based on a White House press release from December which says that since Trump issued Executive Order 13771 (the two-for-one rule), federal agencies have issued 67 deregulatory actions and imposed only three new regulatory actions.

Seems legit, right? Well it would be, if the criteria for regulatory actions and deregulatory actions were the same, or even comparable. But they're not.

A memorandum from the Office of Management and Budget, defines both regulatory actions and deregulatory actions specifically in order to help agencies comply with EO 13771.

The memorandum clearly states that regulatory action means "A significant regulatory action as defined in Section 3(f) of EO 12866", while "deregulatory actions are not limited to those defined as significant under EO 12866"

What does this mean? It means that when you're counting up regulations they've got rid of, you count everything, even things like rules about drawbridge opening timetables, but when you're counting new regulations, you only count the really significant ones. Ones that have a greater than $100 million annual impact on the economy, interfere with multiple agencies, or raise new legal issues.

Attempting to apply the same criteria for both, *Politifact* found that only five deregulatory actions were 'significant', compared to the three new regulations imposed. Right leaning advocacy group *The American Action Forum* looked at only regulations with any economic impact, and found nine deregulatory actions to five regulatory ones.

When you don't compare things fairly, you're not really offering evidence to support your claim.

MORAL EQUIVALENCE

Person A is bad, but Person B is just as bad, so that's OK.

The fallacy of Moral Equivalence is committed when someone argues that because the actions of two people or groups are morally equivalent (whether they are or not), those people or groups are just as bad as each other.

For example, following the Charlottesville white supremacists rally and counter-protest, Trump read a prepared statement. Unfortunately, he went off script for the last few words:

We condemn in the strongest possible terms this egregious display of hatred, bigotry and violence -- on many sides. On many sides.

By ad-libbing 'on many sides' he turned a statement about Nazis into one about both Nazis and the people who were protesting against Nazis. In doing so, he equated a group who chanted Nazi slogans; gave Nazi salutes; carried placards with anti-Semitic slogans; and drove a car into a crowd of people, killing one; with a group who would like it if there were no Nazis.

Three days later, Trump was asked to clarify his remarks, and instead he doubled down, saying:

They didn't put themselves down as neo-Nazis, and you had some very bad people in that group. But you also had people that were very fine people on both sides.

When asked specifically about his 'on many sides' comment, he continued:

Yes, I think there is blame on both sides. You look at both sides. I think there is blame on both sides. And I have no doubt about it. And you don't have doubt about it either.

Even if the level of violence on both sides had been the same, people protesting against fascism are not 'just as bad' as fascists.

MOVING THE GOALPOSTS
(AKA changing the rules, demanding impossible perfection)

> **Person A: X is true because of reason 1**
> **Person B: Here is evidence reason 1 is wrong.**
> **Person A: But X is true because of reason 2**

Moving the Goalposts is such a common tactic that I'm sure everyone has come across it at some point.

When someone makes an argument; you refute that argument with valid logic; and then they move on to a different argument without acknowledging that their first one failed, they've just moved the goalposts.

Sometimes it's even more clear-cut, in that they will set up a specific set of criteria you must fulfill or a specific piece of evidence you must produce to defeat their argument. When that exact goal is met, they will not accept that they are beaten, but instead change the criteria.

This was exactly the situation that arose during Trump's dogged pursuit of Obama's birth certificate to prove that he wasn't born in Kenya.

On The Today Show on April 7, 2011, Trump said:

> *I would like to have him show his birth certificate and can I be honest with you? I hope he can, because if he can't, if he can't and if he wasn't born in this country - which is a real possibility I'm not saying it happened, I'm saying it's a real possibility much greater than I thought two or three weeks ago - then he has pulled one of the great cons in the history of politics.*

On April 27, President Obama did exactly that, making public his long-form birth certificate, providing exactly the proof Trump was asking for.

Naturally, this put an end to the entire 'Birther' movement. Just kidding. Actually, Trump continued to claim Obama was born in Kenya, including a call to *The Situation Room with Wolf Blitzer* when he said:

> *A lot of people do not think it was an authentic certificate*

...efficiently adding an Argument from Popularity to his Moving Goalposts. A few months later he tweeted an unnamed source:

Donald J. Trump ✓
@realDonaldTrump

An 'extremely credible source' has called my office and told me that @BarackObama's birth certificate is a fraud.

1:23 PM - 6 Aug 2012

In fact it wasn't until September of 2016 that Trump finally publicly acknowledged Obama was born in the US, when he devoted the last thirty seconds of a 40 minute press conference to the issue, during which he not only said:

> *President Barack Obama was born in the United States, period*

But also managed to blame Hillary Clinton for the whole conspiracy and take the credit for finishing it.

During his stream-of-consciousness press conference in February 2017, Trump made a bold and very specific claim:

People came out and voted like they've never seen before so that's the way it goes I guess it was the biggest Electoral College win since Ronald Reagan.

Later in the press conference NBC reporter Peter Alexander challenged him, and during the ensuing exchange Trump managed to move the goalposts three times:

Alexander: "Very simply, you said today that you had the biggest electoral margin since Ronald Reagan, with 304, 306 electoral votes. The fact that President Obama got 365 –"
Trump: "Well I'm talking about Republican."

Alexander: "And then President Obama 332, and George H W Bush, 426, when he won as president. So why should Americans trust you?"

Trump: "Well no, I was given that information. I don't know, I was just given that. We had a very, very big margin."

Alexander: "Why should Americans trust you when you accuse the information they receive as being fake, when you're providing information that is fake?"

Trump: "Well I don't know I was given that information I was given I've actually I've seen that information around but it was a very substantial victory do you agree with that?"

NON-SEQUITUR
(AKA does not follow, invalid inference)

X is true because Y=Z

Non Sequitur is Latin for 'does not follow'. Colloquially, non-sequitur tends to be used to mean a sentence which has no relation to the previous one, but in logical fallacy terms, that would more likely be a Red Herring fallacy.

For our purposes, Non-Sequitur describes a situation where the conclusion of an argument appears initially to be related to the premise, but on closer inspection, such a conclusion cannot be drawn from the evidence provided.

At the tail end of 2017, Trump tweeted this masterpiece:

Donald J. Trump @
@realDonaldTrump
Following

In the East, it could be the COLDEST New Year's Eve on record. Perhaps we could use a little bit of that good old Global Warming that our Country, but not other countries, was going to pay TRILLIONS OF DOLLARS to protect against. Bundle up!

4:01 PM - 28 Dec 2017

It's the same argument he's been making since at least 2011:

Basically, the 'logic' goes, it's cold outside - therefore global warming is a hoax. If you try not to think too hard, it kind of makes sense. But then you realize that The Donald is confusing weather with climate, forgetting that 'global' isn't the same as 'New York', and ignoring the science that says climate change will lead to more extreme weather conditions (like, say, the coldest New Year's Eve on record). He's literally citing the effects of climate change in an attempt to debunk climate change.

Simply put, his conclusion does not follow from his premise.

POISONING THE WELL
(AKA smear tactics)

Person A is going to tell you some nonsense about X being false.
Don't listen to him. X is true.

Poisoning the Well is a kind of Ad Hominem fallacy where the attack on the person making a claim happens in advance.

By attributing negative traits to someone before they even have the chance to make their argument, the well poisoner primes the listener not to believe what they are about to hear. As it does not seek to address the actual argument at all, this reasoning is fallacious.

Trump took the opportunity of his speech at the GOP Convention in July of 2017 to poison the well against the Democrats:

So if you want to hear the corporate spin; the carefully-crafted lies; and the media myths; the Democrats are holding their convention next week. Go there.

POST HOC ERGO PROPTER HOC
(AKA questionable cause, confusing correlation with causation)

Y happened after X. Therefore, X caused Y.

Latin for 'after this, therefore because of this', this fallacy is committed when people confuse correlation for causation and assume that because one event followed another, the former was caused by the latter. Of course, while this may be the case, it is by no means certain. The two events may be completely independent for example, or there may be a third element that in fact caused both events.

Trump seems particularly bad at recognizing cause and effect, and is especially prone to taking credit for things simply because they happened after he was elected.

In January 2018 he tweeted one of the most egregious examples yet:

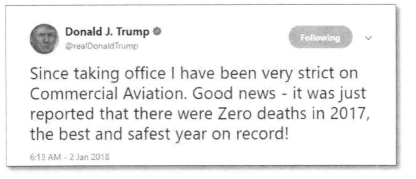

Donald J. Trump @
@realDonaldTrump

Since taking office I have been very strict on Commercial Aviation. Good news - it was just reported that there were Zero deaths in 2017, the best and safest year on record!

6:13 AM - 2 Jan 2018

Trump taking credit for a lack of planes crashing is amazing. Particularly since the increase in safety over the last couple of decades (the last fatal crash of a US passenger plane was in 2009) is largely due to increased regulation - one of Trump's least favorite things.

What has Trump done to increase safety? A quickly rescinded laptop ban for travelers from the Middle East, a proposal to turn air traffic control into a for-profit industry (which never made it through the House) and a failure to appoint both a new FAA administrator, and a nominee for the vacant seat on the National Transport Safety Board. These things are unlikely to be responsible for the safety record.

Of course, Trump being Trump, he doesn't like to keep all the credit for himself. Oh no, wait, yes he does. But at least he can still use the same fallacy to say bad things about Obama. In the 1st Presidential debate in September 2016, he tried to suggest Chicago's homicide rate was Obama's fault:

We have to bring back law and order. In a place like Chicago, where thousands of people have been killed, thousands over the last number of years, in fact, almost 4,000 have been killed since Barack Obama became president.

So according to Trump, Obama took office and then there were almost 4000 gun deaths in Chicago. Sure, he didn't actually say it was Obama's fault - it's difficult following one of Trump's sentences through to a conclusion at the best of times, and this one went on for some time - but the blame was strongly implied.

However, if Trump was serious about playing the Post Hoc Ergo Propter Hoc game, he would see that what actually happened after Obama took office was a dramatic reduction in gun deaths in Chicago. Bill Clinton's presidency saw an average of 769 per year. George W. Bush's saw 533. And Obama's average? 461.

But let's not make the same mistake as Trump and assume this reduction was because of Obama's election. When we look at the statistics we see that it's actually part of a much larger trend. A downward trend in violent crimes, nationwide, since the early 90s.

RED HERRING
(AKA changing the subject, smokescreen, the Chewbacca defense)

X is true because... look over there!

A Red Herring is a distraction, anything that sends a conversation off on a tangent and away from the original point. When someone completely avoids a question by bringing up another issue entirely, they are committing a Red Herring fallacy.

In the 2nd Presidential debate, in October 2016, Trump was asked about the Access Hollywood tape in which he was recorded talking to Billy Bush about grabbing women 'by the pussy'. He responded with one of the most outrageous and blatant Red Herrings in history.

*Yes, I'm very embarrassed by it. I hate it.
But it's locker room talk, and it's one of
those things. I will knock the hell out of
ISIS. We're going to defeat ISIS.*

There wasn't even a pause for breath while Trump changed direction.

At the Democratic convention in 2016, a man named Khizr Khan spoke out against Trump. Mr. Khan's son Humayun was killed serving in Iraq. On *The Week with George Stephanopoulos*, Mr. Trump was asked to respond:

Stephanopoulos: *"He said you wouldn't
have let his son in America".*

Trump: *"He doesn't know -- he doesn't know that. I saw him. He was, you know, very emotional. And probably looked like -- a nice guy to me. His wife, if you look at his wife, she was standing there. She had nothing to say. She probably -- maybe she wasn't allowed to have anything to say. You tell me, but plenty of people have written that."*

Sure, it's uncomfortable when your public opinions about Muslims put you in opposition to a Gold Star family, but if you're Donald Trump you can't just be contrite or, you know, basically decent, so how better to distract from the real issue than by attacking the mother of the fallen soldier? That's a Trump Red Herring special.

SHIFTING THE BURDEN OF PROOF
(AKA onus probandi)

X is true. Prove me wrong.

Typically, the burden of proof lies with the person making the claim. The more outrageous the claim, the more the claimant should be expected to provide evidence before anyone is likely to believe him.

When the claimant instead challenges others to prove his claim is not true he is Shifting the Burden of Proof. This is fallacious because he is not backing up his claim with evidence, or even a logical argument, but simply passing the buck to his opponent. In addition, it is in many cases impossible to prove a negative.

Having made the outrageous claim that more than three million people voted illegally (and all of them for Hillary Clinton, of course), Trump offered no evidence. He did however, retweet a request that journalists prove the opposite:

It seems almost too obvious to say, but millions of people not voting illegally would not leave much evidence behind. If millions of illegal votes had been cast, then we would expect to see some evidence - whether those extra votes came from non-citizens, dead people, or people registered to vote in more than one state, just like Steve Bannon, Jared Kushner, Sean Spicer and Trump's daughter Tiffany.

Voter fraud experts have looked for the evidence, and found none.

SINGLE CAUSE FALLACY
(AKA causal reductionism)

Y (a complex outcome) wouldn't have happened if not for X.

The Single Cause Fallacy is committed when the speaker assumes a complex outcome to have one cause, thereby making it easier to blame on somebody or propose a solution. The reality is that many real-world issues are caused by a combination of factors, some of which may even be too complex for us to be aware of. Oversimplifying issues does not help us to talk about them with reason and logic.

Twitter's decision in late 2017 to expand tweets to 280 characters got a mixed response. Unfortunately, it was inevitable that Trump would use it to make even longer fallacious arguments like this one:

Donald J. Trump ✪
@realDonaldTrump

Following ⌄

People who lost money when the Stock Market went down 350 points based on the False and Dishonest reporting of Brian Ross of @ABC News (he has been suspended), should consider hiring a lawyer and suing ABC for the damages this bad reporting has caused - many millions of dollars!

5:15 AM - 3 Dec 2017

On December 1st, veteran ABC journalist Brian Ross reported that Gen. Mike Flynn would testify that Trump asked him to contact the Russians during the campaign. This was wrong. In fact Trump waited until after the election to ask Flynn to make contact with the Russians.

Trump noted that the stock market dropped 350 points 'based on' this story.
As you can see on this graph, the Dow Jones Industrial Average did indeed drop significantly mid-morning on that day.

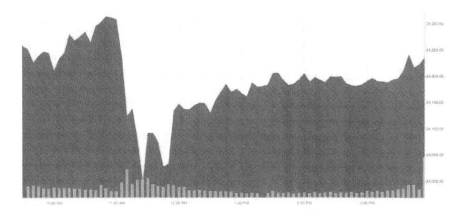

However, it recovered half those lost points within 30 minutes of the drop, and ended the day only 40 points down, despite the fact that ABC News didn't issue a correction to the story until that evening, well after the market had ceased trading.

While the incorrect report may well have been a factor, the stock market fluctuates all the time, and there are many factors that decide the direction and size of fluctuations.

Suggesting this drop is purely due to Brian Ross is to ignore all the other factors, and a considerable oversimplification. By seizing on this aspect of the story, Trump successfully, if fallaciously, drew attention away from the real subject.

At the end of the day, the Dow closed only 40 points down. Over the past 50 years, one day in every three has seen a bigger drop from open to close. This was well within normal boundaries for a day of investing.

SLIPPERY SLOPE
(AKA thin end of the wedge, absurd extrapolation)

If we allow X, what's to stop Y or even Z from happening?

The Slippery Slope fallacy is committed when a person assumes if one bad thing happens, then more, and often worse, bad things will inevitably follow. It is often applied to changes in the law that some groups are campaigning for, and others find distasteful.

It is fallacious because to accept the Slippery Slope argument, you must ignore the possibility that the single change will happen and then everything will calm down unless there is a genuine reason to call for further change.

The events in Charlottesville in August 2017 which ended with clashes between neo-Nazis and anti-fascist protesters, began with a protest about the removal of a statue of Confederate General Robert E. Lee from a public park. While defending the white supremacists several days later, Trump also invoked the Slippery Slope:

Many of those people were there to protest the taking down of the statue of Robert E. Lee. So this week, it's Robert E. Lee, I noticed that Stonewall Jackson's coming down. I wonder, is it George Washington next week? And is it Thomas Jefferson the week after. You know, you really do have to ask yourself, where does it stop?

By using the Slippery Slope fallacy, Trump is ignoring the differences between these people. Washington and Jefferson were famous for many good things they did, and they also owned slaves, as did most wealthy landowners at the time. Lee and Jackson, however, are famous only for fighting a civil war to protect their rights to own slaves. There is no reason to celebrate their legacies that does not involve glorifying slavery.

Removing statues of Confederate Generals for this reason need not lead to removing statues of people who actually achieved something.

Never one to underplay a situation, in March of 2016 Trump tweeted:

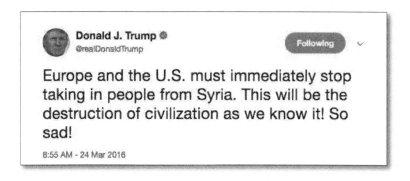

Donald J. Trump ✔
@realDonaldTrump

Europe and the U.S. must immediately stop taking in people from Syria. This will be the destruction of civilization as we know it! So sad!

8:55 AM - 24 Mar 2016

Suggesting if the US and Europe don't immediately stop immigration from Syria, civilization will end? Yeah, that's a Slippery Slope.

SPECIAL PLEADING
(AKA ad hoc reasoning)

Rule X applies to everyone else, but I'm different.

Special Pleading describes a situation where you have a rule that you apply to everyone else, but make up an excuse to explain why the rule doesn't apply to you. When you are inconsistent in applying the rules in this way without a valid logical reason, you are using fallacious reasoning.

In August of 2015, Trump released a campaign position paper entitled 'Immigration Reform That Will Make America Great Again'. In it, he detailed his plan to call for a 'Requirement to hire American workers first':

In the year 2015, with 92 million Americans outside the workforce and incomes collapsing, we need companies to hire from the domestic pool of unemployed.

The only trouble is, over the past 8 years, Trump has hired over 1000 foreign workers on temporary visas to work at his Mar-a-Lago hotel in Palm Beach as cooks, waiters and housekeepers, paying them around $10-12 per hour. How does he justify this? Well, Marco Rubio pointed it out in the 11th Republican Presidential Candidate Debate in March of 2016 and Trump said:

It's very, very hard to get people. But other hotels do the exact same thing. And just so you understand, just again, this is a legal process. This is a procedure. It's part of the law. I take advantage of that. There's nothing wrong with it. We have no choice.

This is clear Special Pleading (with a side order of Tu Quoque). Trump thinks that other people should hire

Americans, but has a spurious reason why that doesn't apply to him. The next day, a press release appeared on Trump's website saying

"I will end forever the use of H1B as a cheap labor program, and institute an absolute requirement to hire American workers for every visa and immigration program. No exceptions."

He followed through on this pledge, signing an executive order in April 2017 which he called 'Buy American, Hire American'.

It didn't stop him from hiring 70 temporary foreign workers at Mar-a-Lago for the 2017-2018 winter season. Is this because there are no Americans with the skills or inclination to do these jobs? Well, in the previous tourist season *BuzzFeed News* talked to a local employment agency. Senior director Tom Veenstra told them he had a database of 1,327 Palm Beach County residents interested in server, cook, and chef positions. He said local hotels were currently seeking his agency's help to fill more than 856 such jobs, but Mar-a-Lago did not appear to be among those that contacted the agency directly.

STRAW MAN

Person A: I believe X (a strong argument)
Person B: See, Person A believes Y (a weak argument)
which I can easily debunk.

When someone makes a strong argument that's hard to refute, don't despair. Simply pretend they made a different argument, that's easier to knock down - you could massively oversimplify what they said, misrepresent the point of their argument, or just put words in their mouth. Congratulations! You've just constructed a Straw Man that's easy to defeat.

The Straw Man fallacy is very common and very effective, particularly in politics. If the audience wasn't really paying attention to what was said, they may be inclined to believe the fallacious re-statement of the argument is a fair representation - especially if it confirms their preconceptions about the speaker.

Trump loves to use the Straw Man fallacy, and his base is inclined to believe what he tells them are the views of his opponents. In June of 2016 in a speech in Redding, CA, he touched on a topic near and dear to the heart of heartland Republican voters:

> *We're going to save our Second Amendment. Hillary Clinton wants to abolish it. Believe me. She wants to abolish our Second Amendment. We're going to save our Second Amendment.*

He repeated the claim at multiple rallies and in front of the NRA.

In fact, Hillary Clinton's views on guns have been publicly stated on many occasions. She is in favor of stricter gun control including universal background checks to prevent guns getting into the hands of criminals. But that's a little harder to argue against than "She's coming for your guns!"

TU QUOQUE
(AKA you too, hypocrisy, two wrongs make a right)

Person A: You did X, which is bad.
Person B: So did you, so it's OK.

Tu Quoque is another Latin one - it literally means "You too." It's a particular type of Red Herring fallacy where the speaker avoids responding to a criticism by distracting the listener with claims that other people (ideally the one doing the criticizing) have also done similar bad things.

It is a fallacy because the original point is not addressed by the response - instead the speaker moves the conversation away from their shortcomings and on to somebody else.

At a press conference in October 2016, Trump was asked why he still hadn't spoken in public about four Green Berets who were killed in an ambush in Niger 12 days before.

Trump explained that he had written letters to the families, but not sent them yet, and that he planned to call later in the week. He then pointed out how awesome he is compared to other Presidents:

> *If you look at President Obama and other Presidents, most of them didn't make calls, a lot of them didn't make calls. I like to call when it's appropriate, when I think I'm able to do it.*

In fact, Obama wrote letters and made calls to families of killed Americans, according to former staffers and Obama's Defense Secretary Leon Panetta. He also met with families at Dover Air Force Base when fallen soldiers bodies were flown home, and frequently visited with wounded troops at Walter Reed National Military Medical Center.

Later in the press conference Trump was questioned on this, and he clumsily backtracked:

I don't know if he did. No no no. I was told that he didn't often... A lot of presidents don't; they write letters. I do a combination of both. Sometimes – it's a very difficult thing to do, but I do a combination of both. President Obama I think probably did sometimes and maybe sometimes he didn't. I don't know. That's what I was told. All I can do is ask my generals. Other presidents did not call. They'd write letters. And some presidents didn't do anything.

At no point did he address the fact that he had gone almost two weeks without acknowledging the deaths of four Green Berets.

The Tu Quoque fallacy doesn't have to be employed purely selfishly. Sometimes you can use it on behalf of a special friend.

Throughout his campaign and Presidency, Trump has assiduously avoided any criticism of Russian President Vladimir Putin. So when Fox's Bill O'Reilly pointed out that Trump shouldn't respect him because *"Putin's a killer,"* Trump leapt to his defense, saying:

There are a lot of killers. What, you think our country's so innocent?

In responding in this way, Trump essentially accepted that Putin is a killer, and tried to distract from this by throwing his own country under the bus.

What he didn't do, was address the assertion that killers, and Putin in particular, are not worthy of respect.

INDEX

Made in the USA
San Bernardino,
CA